PRAYER IN WIND

PRAYER IN WIND

EVA SAULITIS

Book design and layout by Mark E. Cull

Library of Congress Cataloging-in-Publication Data
Saulitis, Eva, 1963–
    Prayer in wind / Eva Saulitis. – 1st ed. – Pasadena, CA : Boreal Books, 2015.
pages cm
ISBN 978-1-59709-443-6 (pbk.)
ISBN 978-1-59709-444-3 (casebound)
I. Title.
PS3619.A948 P73 2015
811'.6—dc23

                              2014916810

The Los Angeles County Arts Commission, the National Endowment for the Arts,
the Pasadena Arts & Culture Commission and the City of Pasadena Cultural Affairs
Division, the Los Angeles Department of Cultural Affairs, the Dwight Stuart Youth
Fund, Sony Pictures Entertainment, and the Ahmanson Foundation partially sup-
port Red Hen Press.

First Edition
Published by Boreal Books
an imprint of Red Hen Press, Pasadena, CA
www.borealbooks.org
www.redhen.org

ACKNOWLEDGMENTS

The roots for this collection go deep and spread wide, from Latvia to Silver Creek, New York, from Alaska to the Big Island of Hawaii. To those places, furrowed into my skin, I give thanks. And to so many who helped along the way, my gratitude—

—to all of my teachers. To Molly Lou Freeman, my first mentor in poetry, my first reader, my first library, my first window into living an artful life. To Peggy Shumaker, mentor in poetry and teaching and generosity and friendship and grace. To Margaret Baker, mentor in living bodily in the world and in the word, mentor in loyalty, in sickness and in health. To John Morgan, mentor in poetry of grief and survival. To my fellow students in the MFA program at the University of Alaska Fairbanks, every one. To my fellow poetry faculty in the University of Alaska Anchorage Low-Residency MFA program, mentors every day: Linda McCarriston, Anne Caston, Elizabeth Bradfield, Derrick Burleson, Zack Rogow, Joan Kane.

—to Elizabeth Bradfield, whose reading of an early draft pulled me up out of process and into poem, and whose insight gave me the book's final shape. And again to Peggy Shumaker, who read the poems aloud to me one unforgettable afternoon at her home on the slope of Hualalai Volcano, so I could finally hear what they were saying.

—to others who listened to and read early drafts of poems, lending an ear or invaluable feedback: Tara Moss, Karla Freeman, David Lynn Grimes, Laura Hendershot, Craig Matkin, Jo Going, Mara Liebling, Wilderness Sarchild, Ron Spatz, Molly Lou Freeman.

—to Jo Going, in whose sanctuary above Homer these poems took hold, in silence, and in communion.

—to Kate Gale and Mark Cull and everyone at Red Hen Press, for saying yes, again and again, for building a true community of writers and readers, for creating gorgeous books, for your spark and energy and artfulness and dedication and passion and for the best damn booth at AWP.

—to the women of Ventspils Writers' and Translators' House in Latvia, where some of these poems were born, and especially to Ieva Balode, who showed me, by bicycle, on foot, and by bus, where I came from, and what language was mine.

—to Joeth Zucco, for her incomparable editor's and artist's eye.

—to my poetry colleagues at the Kachemak Bay Writers' Conference, whose teachings and readings expand my conception of what a poem can do and be, especially James Thomas Stevens, Sherwin Bitsui, Allison Hedge-Coke, Nickole Brown, Camille Dungy, Arthur Sze, Jerah Chadwick, and Olena Kalytiak Davis.

—to the graduate students at the UAA Low-Residency MFA program, where I teach, especially to Kirsten Anderson and Tara Ballard, who invited me to live with their poems and ideas as they finished their thesis work.

—to the work of Christian Wiman, which came into my life at the exact right moment, particularly his prose in *My Bright Abyss*. And to the work of Robert Hass, which showed me how a poem can essay, can reach out far to encompass a world.

—to Wilderness Sarchild, for urging me to write into the worst of it, and beyond.

—to Craig Matkin, the love of my life, who showed me a bog candle. Nothing's been the same since then.

—to my stepchildren, Elli, Lars, and Eve, who, by being so fully alive and awake in the world, bring so much of the world back into my life, and into my poems.

—always, to my sister Mara, whose belief and courage feed and sustain mine. And to my brother (in-law) Jon and my niece and nephews, Phoebe, Sam, and Quinn. Their home has been sanctuary for writing and healing and laughter. At a borrowed desk in their Bainbridge Island guest room, between PET scans and biopsies, I revised this manuscript. And many thanks to Jenn Rusher for the desk.

—to my family, here, there, in the United States, in Canada, in Latvia, survivors all. To the memory of my oma, Veronika Baginskis, my omama, Lucija Ivins, and my tante, Valija Niedra. And to the abiding presence that is my mother, Asja Saulitis.

—to Drs. Lowell Schnipper, Adnan Majid, Julie Gralow, Judy Steyer, Molly Sullivan, Maureen Filipek, Scott Graham, Ruth Bar-Shalom, and to Myrielle Whittle, Hester Hill-Schnipper, Kay Tilton and all the nurses, fellows, technicians, and healers who have cared for me since my cancer diagnosis, doing everything they can to send me, time and again, back into the world, into the wild, into my life.

—to earth.

—to the force that is life on earth.

The following poems previously appeared, often in different versions, in other venues. My gratitude to the editors who gave them homes and to the literary journals that carry on, against all odds. In particular, thanks to Sandra Kleven and Mike Burwell (at *Cirque*) and to Ron Spatz, at *Alaska Quarterly Review*, who has placed many of my Latvian poems and essays, and who asked to see this manuscript early on.

Alaska Quarterly Review, "Prayer 27" (as "Prayer 28"), "Prayer 37" (as "Heaven and the Fallen World"); Alaska State Council on the Arts website, "Prayer 33" (as "Naturalist's Prayer"); *Anchorage Daily News*, "Prayer 11" (as "Facing the Window"), "Prayer 58" (as "Love, Be With Me When I Die"); *Cirque*, "Prelude: After Diagnosis," "Prayer 3," "Prayer 4," "Prayer 48"; *Seattle Review*, "Prayer 28" (as "Memory is All"), and *Sow's Ear Poetry Review*, "Prayer 34" (as "March 20").

for Jo

CONTENTS

PRAYER IN WIND

So while the ashes that rise meet the ashes that fall
I will be the world, for a little while.

—G. C. Waldrep

PRELUDE: AFTER RECURRENCE

The only true wisdom is in knowing you know nothing.—Socrates

As a bird repeats its *dumb luck dumb luck* refrain
I sit staring at steam rising off the darkening pond
of my teacup, realizing after all these years, about him
I know nothing—name, Latin or common, habits
or patterns of migration, swag—wing bars or color at
nape or crown, and that's a shame, all there is to learn
of our shared habits, all I've let flit through the cracks, and now
there's the matter of time. As I try to reckon it, I keep being
distracted—that bird's incessant nattering, the day breeze flapping
wash on the line, the grinding of axles down East End Road,
afternoon light's trill electrical along my arm skin. As the wind
stalking through the screen sets the chimes to clanging,
as my body asserts its imperatives, it's left to only *this*,

only you, my fugitive, my intruder, my real—*teach me*
to pray—I mean—surrender, give over. Today came news,
abstract, unlyrical—*I'm sorry—cells positive for*—a year
or five, who can tell? This I can say with certainty:
the tea is cool, tastes of hibiscus and blackberry.

    The bird is loud.

BOOK I

In Here

All night I rose and fell, as if in water,
grappling with a luminous doom. By morning
I had vanished at least a dozen times
into something better.

—Mary Oliver

PRAYER I

Morning stacked in parallels—inlet,
    flat-topped mountain, cloud strip,

black
    stripe
        of sand. Light arrives in threads
at nine, faint as scent marks. This is the hour

    before *I want there to be*, before prayer,
any *please, God*: just a mountain dusted in pale

blue talc. That's all.
That's enough.

    Before any *if*, a tree

in deep winter, north of here,
laying down its shadow-lace,
and someone walking away

memory I peel

off moonlit snow and carefully
glue to this incipient
    sky, line by line.

Lay it down like a wing track.
Until a soul can't hold

any longer, and cracks, crying its tiny *please*,

(the way birdsong bursts into daylight):

please don't let anything
begin or be
just yet, please
day, don't arrive for me.

—11.28.2012

PRAYER 2

No one wants another paean to a rosy dawn,
so it's good this one's bluish, baby-shade
at the horizon, bleeding up into midnight like
a botched dye job.

And having enough of the old world—larks,
crakes, nightingales, storks—this space
is populated by one fly crabbing
across a notebook page. He seems, like me,

honey-slowed by winter's shortest days, clumsy
and isolated. My love bought a black-and-white
photo once, close-up of a birch trunk,
fly crawling up

the curled paper bark, marring the purity
of the image. You don't notice the fly
until you do, and then you can't stop.
No one wants a fly in art,

but there it is, elegantly framed.
And we're over the epic, so here, first thing
this morning, a pedestrian quarrel. Years ago, I flew
across a mountain range in black coat

and black boots to secretly meet him
in the city. How many dawns did it take to arrive
at this particular? At 9:30 the sky flares
not like flame—a paper fan

you buy in Chinatown for a dollar.
A sudden breeze sways the Tibetan flags strung along
the eaves. I never noticed how thin
the fabric. You can see right through the printed prayers

to the thermometer—
five degrees—and beyond, birches leaning
all to windward. Sun bleaches out
the last mysterious. Now we pray to the real.

                                        —11.29.2012

PRAYER 3

This morning I remember the one who talked
to the radio—I was building a church
out of Lincoln logs, legs akimbo on the rag rug, singing
in a mixed-up language baubled with the invented, the broken
Latvian, the accented, the foreign: pinecone— *čiekurs*, priest—
mācītājs. Determined girl who ventured alone to Mass
one Sunday, unwatched by Father (distracted by
his schnapps and cigarettes, his playing cards).
The one who crossed four lanes to get there,
shouldered the heavy door open, her small voice calling
Mama. Hallowed be the child, palming green apples to
the abused mare, girl still shocked and scared
after finding the corpse
of the blue heron her brother nailed
to the ash. Ash Wednesday, forehead smudged, marked for
obliteration. Born into immigrant pain, which is peasant, Gregorian. I pray
for the girl who prayed for God to take her sister's migraine
and give it to her, exclaimed later, in her journal, *And I think
he did*. Sweet-sad sin-eater, for her, this atomic
sunrise smoking through spindles of trees, for her of misguided
faith, the reckless unmarred predawn too-long dark before
she wakes, before doubt or shame, this wind chime,
for her, slivers of light caught in twists of birch bark, tangled
in the lint of the woolen table runner. For her hand-built
church—this cold winter wood.

—11.30.2012

PRAYER 4

Two years past that day I jogged down
the hospital steps, burned red
by radiation, certificate of completion
crumpled in my fist, the hush
and mute unmusical shades
of smoke-blue and terror,
slight suggestion of grace. Since then
tea cup never empty, sky never not
in flux.

I sit at the kitchen table watching
light's slow dissolve of a dark
beyond fathoming, a neighbor's truck lights inching
down the iced-up lane. Oblong cloud a violent
flush at ridgeline. All squandered, 730 dawns
wolfed down since that one.

Earth, what shall I want? To be set down in a frozen
pasture, to be snatched up by
a great gray owl?
Light streaks east, flapping her giant
flagrant wing.

That it be benign,
that it be forgiving.

—12.1.2012

PRAYER 5

1.

The ridgeline hones its blade
against first light. Nine degrees. Unmitigated
by a single cloud, the cold
deep and Baltic.

My oma prayed all the waking
hours, mild or frozen. Crumbling
in her lap, cover warped and wrapped
in wrinkled wax paper, her devotional.
Twined around her fist, rosary of crude
wood beads. In a peasant tongue,
she rocked us.

2.

Her name was Veronika. Back to her
I trace my root—altar, hymn, prayer card,
folk Mass, tarot deck, medicine wheel, superstition,
I Ching, smudge stick, Virgin of Guadalupe. To her
I ascribe my peasant ways—pitchfork, compost
heap, potato patch, sorrel blades busting up
through a blanket of mulch. Sorrel's lemon
tang on my tongue—host of hosts.
All the ways I pray.

3.

Oma bore seven sons,
four daughters, in the log
sauna on the farm. One girl
drowned in a water trough,
another died of sickness. One son,
hips dysplastic, crawled a mile
along a dirt track to Mass.
Swore if he walked back,
he'd become a priest.
By the time the war came,
that son was ordained.
Another son ordained himself
Waffen SS soldier. He became
my father. A boy, he played priest
to the fowl and cattle,
a man, made us kneel
on a hardwood floor
as penance. Or knee to knee
with him in the basement, one
rosary to share. His open palm
or closed fist or belt buckle
or birch switch psalming down
and down upon us—
Lord, hear our prayer.

4.

There's an impossible way
peach elides into blue, then
deepens, healing into daylight,
and the temperature rises.
There's a way a mountain range
frees the sky of its inks
and holds them in its care,
a living cargo of darkness
that made us.

—12.2.2012

PRAYER 6

after writings of Lorca

When he says *all one knows is that it burns the blood like powdered glass*
is that the same glass scattered on the floor of your ruined farmhouse,
Veronika? Were the gunshots and creakings of wagon wheels
your rusty knives? And when he says it *surges up from the soles
of the feet*, is that what surged down from you, squatting in the sauna,
pushing, pushing your infants out? Surging down the creek bed of
your body, the afterbirth, into the heat and steam, out from your mouth
the dark sounds, animal cries when you buried each girl by the spring?
I have looked for you, Veronika. Once, in the dark, a child, I hid
as you undressed and revealed the folk song of your flesh. I've traveled
far in search of you under the kerchiefs of crones rocking on pews.
In the village square among grandmothers, thick ankled, stout, walking
their Soviet-era bikes, baskets loaded with radish and kraut. In fields,
where a woman bent at the waist to harvest turnips was not you, I held
your earth's red sugar in my hands. Veronika, when Lorca says
that the listeners *tore their clothes rhythmically when she sang*, is that
what you did, beating your chest with your fist when you prayed
for those lost girls, for your war-bound son? By rote, you repeated
the rosary's round, thorny sonnet crown for your offspring: peasants,
priests, soldiers, beekeepers, maids, one librarian. When Lorca claims
it's a nation of death, I don't have to ask. It's your peasant *duende*
he's talking about, rising off the fresh-turned earth, up from the soles
of the feet of women hoeing fields, out from their mouths the ancient
songs born of a place where every wheel is broken or mired, every ruin's
a nest for doves, every word is tired, nearly dead, but it fills the mouth—
bitter, like your beer, your black bread.

—12.3.2012

PRAYER 7

Same wrung stones not yielding a drop
of honey. Candles burning to nubs
before the same sun clears the ridge. Same raw
material lacking luster. This particular dawn
redundant, mere, and echoey. Studded by same
thought-bubbles, mind's same oatmeal. Chewed-off
like the ear of a frozen hare in a dog's mouth, same
search pattern yielding same result. Black trees
saming selves against black sky. Never
the surprise— owl, lynx, coyote, bear—always
a snowshoe hare girdling a rose bush. Same gear-grind,
Monday his truck up then down the icy road, schlepping
its load of trouble. Same light froth at 10:00 a.m., maybe two
minutes slower in arriving. Same waiting for auto-reply
to same question, same planks planking
the same old barn. Same shadows jumbled
together on lawn. From mountain and breaking
sun, same refusal to praise or damn.

—12.4.2012

PRAYER 8

some dawns the curtains stay drawn and no one's praying,

some mornings it's all we can do to put on

our coats, start up our cars to warm them

we've got it wrong—prayers are out there

being prayed, just not by our kind—crunch

of snow crust —some lord, a moose, or just the cold,

settling deeper

—12.5.2012

PRAYER 9

As if this time of day were the ornate cupboard
at the back of the church with its maroon
velvet drape, as if light arriving reveals
the opaque fishiness of an old priest's face.
As if this blush along the ridgeline were shame,
as if the pew, this hard wooden chair, as if
this repetition, my last confession
being yesterday morning, as if this catechism,
each dawn, the scalloped ridge reconfiguring,
light galloping renegade behind
black candles of trees.

If wind is belief, throwing its weight, if
the sky is a soul's exact
replication, if I am pulling back
the curtain, slipping in to ask
for absolution, if the soul were not
already wiped clean, if forgiveness
didn't happen like winter, unmediated, if
the soul didn't simply get happened upon
like a day—marred
by sun, clouds, hues, one degree or two
of temperature sharpening in all directions,
if an owl's wing prints on snow weren't all
the mercy we're given.

                              —12.6.2012

Morning opens like a suitcase. Gaping
on the floor, half-empty of its contents: wool
leggings, turtlenecks, granola bars. Everything
held in abeyance by a mandarin glow over
mountains and in north-facing
purple shadows. No wind yet ruffling
the fabrics, scarves, sleeves, hems
of dresses, silks of camisoles spilling onto
frozen ground. Sunrise is long, hours to unpack
what's been given. A penniless musician
tells me he walked into town enacting a new song
that goes, *I'm gonna love myself and you at the same time*. Daylight
reveals to each its own particular conundrum. I love
the stand of spruce outside the window. I love the moon's
crooked smile in the velveteen where night still lingers—
and God—unequally, and not at the same time.

—12.7.2012

PRAYER II

A network of branches crazes
the sky like cracks in the glaze
of a Chinese cup. Dawn, a poised
dropper. History poised also. A man
on the street corner waves his sign:
Germany 1934. So cold, elbows of trees
creak when something flaps by—
the *craw craw craw*—

Would I be able to recognize places
in Latvia by my father's absence—
farmyard littered with dented milk cans,
mattresses leaking straw, table set
for a meal that never happened?

Every morning I look out a window
at a scene he wouldn't recognize,
blue tide of sunrise spreading west
obliterating tracks of satellites,
gray tide of inlet shoring up
the wrack-line.

My father steps through his window.
He's put on his SS uniform.
He stands on a dirt road, staring toward
the vanishing point where the past is rectified.
The first thing I heard this morning— three
harsh cries— was the black crow veering

past his head. *History,*
welcome back, it said. I watch to see
what he does next.

—12.8.2012

PRAYER 12

Oboe of the violet twilight, contrapuntal
to rain on the roof, temperature rising while
the gale descending erases the mountain, wipes
out sunrise. World as close-up—wind-lick
of grasses, how they brush their faces against
the earth's white drumskin. Unable to tell
when day begins, we dim the lights,
my friend and I on the window seat in wool leggings
listening to Brahms, say nothing. Some mornings
ask of us a shepherding in. Some, a requiem.

—12.9.2012

In the interval between fog turning blue and fog turning gray, a lot can happen.

On the floor my friend leaves her roadmap open, an orange mark sinuous and

certain as a bass line charting her way to Banff. I imagine her white truck rattling

over the Alcan's washboard, mantle aurora haze to the north, the breath

of some celestial convoy she's racing. The day softening into being, I am looking

for something similar to firmly press my marker to a page and say *yes, that way*.

Instead this bone-deep fog-ache caught in the trees, this flux between states of being

and not being, the crepuscular way night exits

one particle at a time. Her truck

packed with easels, brushes, watercolor paper, my friend departs at daybreak

to follow a map of definite desire that isn't mine, not for the wanting. I drive off

in the opposite direction—west, then north, then south through freezing rain.

Road glare flashes back the car's lights and shadow, and ice is falling

a quarter inch an hour—wintry mix I'm escaping, but reluctantly, muttering my

from-the-foxhole *please God*, please. I pull over for a breather at the Hope cutoff, a plow truck slows, a guy leans across his seat, up-thumbing, eyes a-questioning,

and I mouth *I'm good, thanks.* And I am, at last seated in the exit row, sewing

a button on a sweater I won't need for months, waiting for take-off, waiting for

someone else—stranger is best—to navigate. Look, there's a human being

on a cherry picker shoveling a foot of snow off the plane's wing with a push broom.

—12.10.2012

BOOK 2

A Ways Out There

and thou, Blessed One,
smiling with immortal countenance,
didst ask What now is befallen me,
and Why now I call,

and What I in my mad heart
most desire to see.

—Sappho, from "Fragment 1"

PRAYER 14

Teach me, teach me, teach me shrieks
the myna at the first dawn-sliver
above the ocean on the first morning.
Nest-hole thief, invader, I didn't ask for
this, your black claws scratching the roof tin,
you didn't ask for me.

—12.11.2012

PRAYER 15

December 21, 2012, was regarded as the end-date of a 5,126-year-long cycle in the Mayan calendar. Scenarios suggested for the end of the world included the arrival of the next solar maximum, an interaction between Earth and the black hole at the center of the galaxy, or Earth's collision with a planet called Nibiru.

On their last day alive, some do yoga at dawn on concrete
ruins of a railroad depot, feral cats slinking between
their down-dog legs. Some get drunk. Some push sugar cane
through a grinder, hand you a glass of sweet nectar. Some folks
prepare assiduously, stockpiling water and cans of Spam. Some
business goes on as usual, the stock market, for example, and
fracking, Takata's grocery, and armed robbery.

The fudge shop sells fudge, the kava bar, kava in coconut shell bowls.
Some hippies down bowl after bowl until they stop worrying
about the end-times. One picks up a ukulele and everyone sings
through numbed lips. Some old man with a worn canvas pack
slung over his shoulder pauses to quiz a couple checking email
outside the kava bar. *Really? Is this what you're choosing?* Others wield
chainsaws and power drills and weed-whackers, and some say
they'll be over tonight with bells on. Some people spend money at Costco
and Walmart, and some at galleries, shelling out $100 for four
Japanese tea bowls. Me, on my last night, I dream an enormous plane
drifts over the house, silently plummets to earth, registers
its end as sparks along the electric fence. From a black canal,
survivors emerge, two boys and a girl, dripping, grieving
for nothing, calm as through just born. I kneel
to pull in their small surrenders.

—12.21.2012

PRAYER 16

"Make a fist for the heart," a poem says.
What I want to know first off is, offense
or defense? If the heart grew a fist, would it
wield its heart stuff more mightily?
Would it love madly, care less for propriety or
politeness, for who's and who's not
invited? If a heart fist, brass-knuckled,
led the parade, how high could I hurl
this baton, how fast twirl? No ifs.
Missing you, its clench undeniably strong.
Look at me here wrenching the fingers apart
to start this day. Dead is the peaceful
heart, the one whose thirst is quenchable.
Alive heart fist is the fresh
wound-parch on your face, Christmas Day.

—12.25.2012

PRAYER 17

Sometimes the physics of wind defines outcomes:
laundry hung on the line, whether a T-shirt
wraps into a cocoon or flaps like an injured
bird or dangles. I am trying to meditate, and I am distracted
by this dubious insight, as well as by my love
watering eggplants, an orange tractor parked outside.

So let this be a prayer for the war(p) between

 a world lived on the page, in the mind, and another, of wind,
 'ō'ō bar, pickax, bleach. And in memory, singing in the choir loft, Our Lady
of Mt. Carmel, Lucille at the pipe organ, the opening mouths and chords
of *Let there be peace on earth, and let it begin with me* constructing
a mosaic of leaves and debris. I am leaving now, to load
the dehydrator with bananas, to fill holes in the ground
with cassava and pigeon pea. I am going outside to wield my shovel.

—12.27.2012

PRAYER 18

We listen to the two-beat whistle of the last
coquí frog left awake, pause to ponder
lava casts of trees burnt up in flows
two centuries past.

A man in a torn T-shirt jogs around
and around the path, another smokes
ganja in the pagoda.

Are we having
a spiritual experience
yet? You might ask

the 'ōhi'a seedling, sprouting from the lava tree's
brow furrow. The fern emerging
like a flaming
stigmata from a burn hole.

The eye sockets
of an incinerated forest,
from which this tendril grows.

—12.28.2012

PRAYER 19

One day of the old year left, I drink green tea, consider my options.
How does anyone change? I know nothing, but I keep going.

The island knows about change: sandalwood, then sugar cane.
Cow pasture, then Christian camp. Mission school, then mac nut farm.

The dream keeps elaborating: a barn, a house, a yard. As a syringe
ploughs into the skin, someone else's vision of earth as heaven.

When I close my eyes I see a gulch bright with green, heart-shaped leaves,
a triangle of ocean between two cliffs. A naked woman treads water.

Her fluttering hands like the dorsal fins of angel fish, she's not me, she's
the place I'm supposed to be going, my resolution. Trade winds push

clouds down the chain, dropping skeins earthward. Near the sheep pen,
a hibiscus responds, opening more blossoms. Ocean wedged

and trenched by wind, whitened where the propeller cuts in,
the oldest heaven lies just beyond reach, this earth's next iteration, and mine.

—12.31.2012

PRAYER 20

Not to mention dreams, his and mine
corresponding around epic water. In his, our house
wiped out by tsunami, in mine, a pool in which
I'm swimming naked among parents and tots, shocking them
with my mastectomy scar. Not to mention him
shoveling dirt right outside my window
when I'm toiling for quiet. Not to mention
it's already afternoon, and maybe that's why
I sound flippant. Not to mention I skipped
meditation. Not to mention the bossiness
of ducks who peck my shins when I fill
their water trough and the truculence
of geese who open their beaks, unfurl
their tongues and hiss, demanding more
corn, and faster. The rude world doesn't wait
for inspiration, it goes hurling itself at fragile seedlings,
spitting its gobs like buck-toothed alpacas,
adorable-appearing, but mean.

—1.3.2013

PRAYER 21

This is a prayer for the waste, days, hours
badly spent, forays into the internet jungle-land
of links from the launch of the words *symptoms*
of recurrent breast cancer. For tangled sheets, and novels
whose plots are long lost, for staring at ceilings in the dark,
trying not to blink. For wasted fivers at coffee shops
or newsstands waiting for delayed flights. For Scrabble,
the weather underground, www whatever dot com, for
catalogs. Trying sweater after earring, convincing myself
I require new shoes and a more neutral color palette.
For staring out the window waiting for dawn, or the mail truck,
or the right line. For lingering near the duck pond
for no good reason. Arranging books alphabetically and
by size. To what end? For cleaning, wiping counters
of someone else's crumbs and butter smears. Cooking
by recipe, generally, an excuse not to be doing something
hard. And hey, why are those trees just standing there?
Bum birds hitched to their bum limbs. Wind blowing
their errant leaf tinsel and what-nots. Everything waiting
for the cows to come home, when they won't, ever.
They're cows, and need to be driven.
This is a love poem for the cows.

—1.4.2013

PRAYER 22

Trade winds gusting fifty wake us before dawn, so now
we're fiddling with the window's wooden louvers. Certain gusts
whistle through any slit but for those that drum the metal roof, no
solution. True this island's rooted, and we can't keel or
broach. Besides, wind wants only to chase itself westward,
means no ill will, or benevolence. Stripped leaves, tumbling
Styrofoam, toolsheds imploding and scattering
recycling and outboard parts across lava fields—unintended
consequence. Like hormones sweeping unbidden through
a young boy's veins, leaving a hickey, which he can't explain.

—1.7.2013

PRAYER 23

Fear triggers
most prayers. Fear, and one
black egg laid in the banana grove
of my dream life. One glossy
black hen crossing a gulch
to get here, all night long,
her witless task. When in the dream
I held her gift to light, I realized
it was the color of certain
lavas, black-infused maroon,
but translucent. On New Year's
Eve, we walked to the bluff edge, watched
a lemon-skinned moon
bob like a dumpling over
the cove. A lighthouse beamed
its charisma across our shirt fronts,
a child cried *moon, light, we.*
Someone older chanted *down,*
down, down to the sea, and I
remembered a song teaching me
about skiing: you *kick, kick,*
and then you glide. I felt it there,
the egg, so wasn't quite present
to all that transpired. Only now, here,
half-awake, recalling, I suspect
that's how most of life goes,
flowing, flowing, down to
the sea. The kind of radar I used
to find one black egg among
fallen banana leaves would be

useful now, in daylight. The goose
flared her wings and hissed
at the curious child. My father used
a birch switch. Memory, not dream,
is responsible for this. Each egg
ungathered, an unexploded shell
that will propel us backward.

—1.8.2013

PRAYER 24

Sun flare on the bay like a dime on a platter.
The silver one my grandmother buried in the farmyard
in Latvia before she fled, told Tante Līna to unearth after

the war. Tarnished, pitted, the treasure distressed, for that,
worth more. In the box later there was no platter,
just a few oddities Līna sent to America: gray blanket

trimmed with pink—Latvian patterns someone worked
into the weave, snowflakes, stars—and one towel.
Use it, my mother said, until it's one big stain. Chipped

like grandmother's teacups, ripped like her afghan,
cracked like her pendant. In the end repurpose it
for the dog bed. No saving china shards in a paper sack

for some tile project. No virtue, no art in hoarding
broken bits for memory's sake. When I was a kid she was
nostalgic. Once to sew a doll's dress I took scissors

to my grandmother's blouse for the lace and my mother
wept. Now, she rifles through closets, drawers, jewelry
box, thrusts every saved thing at us, says take it.

The winter platter on the bay busts through
nostalgia like a fist. And I'm standing beside Līna
who's wearing a gray dress, hem dirt-stained. It's 1946.

Her headscarf wet with sweat, she leans
on a shovel, having a smoke, just for me she's digging
for silver beneath the field, jabbing the blade

at a crust of frozen sod. Sorry for the trouble, I say
I'll treasure it. She says *Don't be stupid,* kicking the loam
with her boot, chucking her cigarette. *It's time. Use it.*

—1.9.2013

PRAYER 25

Today is my day to study the Zen
of greed. It starts with the creep
of my hand across the coverlet, lifting

the sheet so as not to disturb my
loved one's sleep. Eager for the heavy
dew on the orchard grass, to have it

all to myself, for my feet alone to fashion
my dark memos in that grass. The leak of light above
the Kohala Mountains I do not wish

to share with anyone. I whistle
for the dog. Spot my neighbor hosing
his plants against the depredations

of Chinese beetles, barefoot, in his night
clothes. I stash his image away and
now I lay it down on the table, beside

the others I pocketed—wild turkey
pair ambling past the avocado. It's like
a weird tarot, or a kid sorting and counting

her trick-or-treat hoard. Innocently,
my lover fills a feeder outside the kitchen
window, and now the Java sparrows spar

and chir, spitting epithets at the Brazilian
cardinals. By afternoon, they've devoured
every blessed seed. I pull a card

at random from my Zen deck, get *nothingness*,
and dissatisfied, pull another: *nothingness*
again. I think I'll go out this afternoon

and try to capture the good light, take my selfie,
post it on Facebook, or just carve
into the trunk of a tree: *I was here.*

Yes, it was me. I was first, I took
the eggs, the ripest mango, my greed
holy, limitless.

—1.10.2013

Why? Why is a crooked letter, my mother-in-law used to say. She held
no truck with useless inquiry, superstition. Buck up. Be present. *Suffer*

no fools, no dogma. When she died, I sleuthed her shelves. She read
everything—Buddhist philosophy, AARP magazine, *The Art*

of Loving, Hawaiian poetry, books on aging, Asian painting,
and dying. She stopped just short of a PhD in English lit, took acting. No

shrinking violet, she wore tennis whites on Sundays, permed and dyed
her hair various reddish shades, waited for her husband weekdays with

wine glasses frosted in the deep freeze. *You little ingrates, wait till your*
father gets here. Protested his pollarding of her ornamental trees

in the garden. A closetful of peacock-hues to counter his muted same-same.
Years after he died, we found the glasses, the bottle of cream sherry still

frozen. She never gave his clothes away. *You better know how to laugh*
at yourself, she said. Afraid she'd take me for the shrinking violet, the

suffering fool, tucked into the shade of a summer day, *why,* my crooked
angel, I kept quiet, secretly studied her tracings, finger along the spines of books

and facts. Her sons sang her past the last breath, hospital bed on
the living room's shag. In the mail we got her Hiroshige prints, a 1950's lamp,

a volume of bad Hawaiian poetry, costume jewelry, one conundrum—wooden
statue of mother Mary praying. To her tough and inscrutable hide, I offer up this day.

—1.11.2013

PRAYER 27

Imperfect birds, saffron finches, they don't hail
from here, but from South America, where, caged,
the males are used for blood sport. Two girls
for every boy, and territorial to boot, troopers,
they take to it. Tanagers, like the scarlet of my youth,
(my mother loved them at the feeder, *look, look*, pointing,
tan-en-jers, the r rolled). She said also li-no-*lay*-um.
Traders-Joe. Nut-hatcher. Other Latvianisms. To pray
is to follow one word to its next, a pilgrimage, a trail
of seeds, crumbs, or dead grass, which saffron finches
hoard for nests. A pinch of precious saffron threads
heated in a pan of milk yellowed my mother's kliņģeris,
braid of yeasted, golden-raisin-studded bread for
our name's days. From memory to philology, the trail
goes. But the saffron finch has its story too, and I don't
know how it arrived, in whose cage or breast pocket, upon
which storm or consequence. Considered common, tolerant
of us, itself displacing native birds. No surprise, being lovely,
with its tangerine face as though dipped in the fruit's bleeding
rind. My mother arrived by boat, the *General Sherman*, she
was raped by another immigrant. Never lost her accent,
never perfected English, for sixty years, never told
anyone. Said to her daughters only, from you, men just
want_____. We filled in the rest.

—1.16.2013

PRAYER 28

for Ralph

Preparing for Kona winds, we pound
poles into soil at the base
of Buddha belly bamboos, the old *hamii*.

We tether the green flexing canes
to pickets of dead bamboo,
give them form, tell them bend

this far and only this. Make a screen
for us on this little ridge. Be our
windbreak, heal our eyesore. All day

leaves and birds jabber in gusts. Caught
in the cloudburst our backs get wet.
Places have memories. It scares us

to think so. I am like bamboo, placeless,
transplanted someplace new, staked
to withstand foreign weather. But I

remember. We pause in our work, turn
our faces up to rain, our open mouths, one
after one. We think desire is enough.

It's not. We build our privacies, impenetrable,
thin. We want places to remember us.

—1.18.2013

PRAYER 29

I used to think when I died—I could see you—
so I died as fast as I could—

but that was juvenile, now I don't. I mean,
don't romanticize as much, or even claim to know
what or who you are, so I write as though you were
corporeal, outside my window, within shouting distance:
dear weed-whipper, dear breeze, dear heat, dear rumble
from the sea that unnerves, dear heaven, dear hell, dear task-
master, dear tractor, dear never, dear streambed, dear runoff,
dear dream of tunnel, dream of white gosling the size of an ostrich
rejected by its mother, dear thirsty hen racing for the muck pond.
I am writing to you from my empty cup, my book with dog-eared
pages, a coffee stain, the cloy of jackfruit in my nose, morning light
on manila envelopes, sprung rat trap, rat-chewed soap, unplayed
oboe, what you call sloth, the weather dry yet mellow, a drought but
the tourists are pleased, dear longing, dear jerk butting into
my business, dear cowboys unlocking the gate.

I saw their ponies tethered to a trailer, heads low slung,
black tails swishing, the image of endurance, western
saddles outfitted with quirts and rope coils before I saw
the cowboys themselves, and they weren't smiling, those
cowboys were not made for TV, they had cows to move, work
to do, no time for a chat, I was no one to them, as I am no one
to you. See how I see you in everything. See how I want—
you—everything. See how I make you
all about me. Dear no one, why don't you
answer, or understand, dear distance, dear gulch,
dear continent, please write, forgive me, most sincerely,
your servant, your friend.

—1.21.2013

Jess brought the lamb down to the farm, orphan
she'd shorn, white hair she'd shampooed so it bristled
like an old marine's brush cut. Pink showed through
at ear and underbelly, the nascent udder. The lamb,
used to the bottle, the nuzzle against Jess's neck, now
nibbles kamani leaves, dead electric fence wire,
testing everything for a living current. Jess lingered,
reluctant to leave the lamb she'd nursed, kept tethered
in her dead father's backyard for months. Half-orphan
herself at twenty, she lives in his house, painted the kitchen
plum, works at Holy Bakery rolling out pie crusts. She delivered
the lamb collared, leashed, and now it bleats, blundering
through the pasture, bumping into other sheep, as though
perplexed. *What am I?* When it ducks the wire, wanders
onto the lawn, the farmer smacks its rump, yells, *go on,*
you're a sheep. The flock grazes in the lower pasture, nickering,
be one of us. The lamb resists, lies alone under the ironwood.
I sit here distracted by her nonstop bleating, but do nothing
because they don't understand trouble, do they, the animals,
not like us.

—2.3.2013

PRAYER 31

Purple sash above the island, mauve ad nauseam.
Rain now, torrents squalling down. Then silence, drips.
Relentless, the beginnings, the ends. The irrelevant
data points streaming between magnetic poles
that keep reversing. You can't stop observing,
as you do the forming of a blood blister
on a hammered thumb. It will hurt like hell later,
but you watch, you let it come.

—2.6.2013

PRAYER 32

Wind blows west thirty-five knots
for days, scouring two thousand miles
of uninterrupted ocean. They call it trades,
but I call it father-in-heaven, indifferent passage
brushing our house walls in the darkness.
Last night it drovered blue clouds,
herded the moon and shadows before it.
It doesn't care one whit about us,
not to shake a stick or bend an ear, or lord
it over, or hear any prayer, and yet, barefoot
on the porch before bed, I find it not so
cowboy lonesome. How good to be
overlooked tonight, un-knocked about
by wind's ministrations, the shit happenings
that happen when father-in-heaven
pauses, pays attention. Tonight I'm nothing,
like banana trees, stars, wolf spiders. We could trade
names and places. The wind doesn't know me from a hole
in a tree or a termite in a house piling, much less
Eve or Adam. Tonight, the wind makes me glad,
not afraid, to be so thoroughly forgotten.

—2.25.2013

BOOK 3

Further

>   *Blessed*
> *be the dust. From dust the world*
> *utters itself. We have no other*
> *hope, no knowledge.*
>   *The word*
> *chose to become*
> *flesh. In the blur of flesh*
> *we bow, baffled.*

>   —Denise Levertov

PRAYER 33

for Alces

I want to place my hands on either side

      of her face, pull her head toward mine, turn it, stare

         into one eye at a time.

I want to trace the frost line of her lash, lick it off my fingertip.

I want her breath to sweat my neck, her lips to nuzzle

      my throat like it's

         a willow branch.

I want to stroke the flour scoops

      of her ears.

I want to press my ear to her waist.

I want to track her careful steps through March snow, ponder

      the kindness of her bony knees, lie in

      her daybed all night long.

Today I collected

      the wiry hairs wild rose snags

from her winter coat,

       secreted them in my jacket pocket.

Today her feral on my hands.

I want her secretly

     to study me. I want to be seen

      by a wild thing.

Please look at me.

               —3.14.2013

PRAYER 34

Light stumbles
down the road, briefly
observed through a thickness
of trees. In the ravine, the dank
lingers, that disarranged cleft
gathering a handful
of nothing.

But it feels futile. If this poem . . .
if this day . . . outside the window,
a hummingbird splay winged
like Blake's fallen angel.

Ten years ago, we went to war.
Then, as now, after rain, in the desert,
ocotillo blooms from green
fingertips. God's fingernails turn
flamenco red, point up,
toward heaven.

A boy says, "Let's throw
down our angers," he gathers
rocks, chucks them off
a ridge in Anzo Borrego. Look

how they break up, get smaller
as they career down
into the wash, take out
a barrel cactus.

Back in Orange, it's foggy
with a jangly
breeze. The tingle-
tangle of washed-out
light through serrated blades
of some xeric shrub. Stub
of a limb. I remember
the image. In the haze
above Baghdad, a sickly flare,
a rock rose, as frail, as capable
of crumbling.

—3.20.2009/3.20.2013

PRAYER 35

Just over your oncologist's shoulder
a door to a place he can't see,
scene he can't enter, you lying

face down under a stunted
hemlock twisting toward a blot
of sun. Nose buried in sphagnum

moss, eyelashes wet with antiseptic
earth-seep, you press your naked
need to a living bandage. Detritus

clings. Your ear throbs. While eye to eye
with him, listening to the odds,
tumor grades & markers, ponds,

dark & multiple, tense, not to pathology,
ontology of *metastatic*, but a different
weight, dimpling of beetle feet,

water striders, your trailing
inklings & the touchdown, briefly,
of mated dragonflies. Beyond intake

& breath-hold & eye-lock, beyond
your consent, his *Godspeed*, you hear it,
the bog's answering gasp—sound

of a machine that, in moments
like these, does your breathing for you.

—4.1.2013

PRAYER 36

Vertical slats of light inch up
cottonwood bark, the ground
white and hard, someone yesterday
drove a truck across the lake,
left wet tread marks. No angels

perch in treetops, just seeds
yet to drop. Moths wobble across
the window glass on frozen wings.
No singing, just the hopeful
hum of a Beechcraft descending
toward the airstrip. If there's a burning
sign, it's ducked behind
a cloud. Tonight it will be
ten degrees.

On the sill, one orchid stalk,
blossom by blossom, dying
toward its tip. Like the chill that crept
up from my father's feet to his legs,
at the last. Another orchid
extends a budding spike toward
November's poverty of daylight.
This is what the dying do.

—11.4.2013

PRAYER 37

To stand in the woods and watch
the St. John's Day fire, the Latvians holding glasses
of schnapps, to stand in the woods unseen,
to watch the women in knee-length
skirts, in pantyhose and pumps, the men stripped
of their ties and jackets. To see them
again, Mr. and Mrs. B, oak leaf wreaths crowning
their heads, leaning against each other
and singing *līgo, līgo,* as if nothing's happened.

As if Mr. B had never collapsed dead
at his carpentry bench, as if Mr. K had never
discovered the spot on his lung. To see the men light
each other's smokes between songs, light them from
their own burning ends, tossing the butts into the fire.
To see anorexic Mrs. K crunching almonds
snuck from her pocket. As if she still had a stomach.
To see her again in her tan pantsuit, the amber
rings loose on her fingers, as if she still had limbs.

Like there's no tomorrow, the men heave
more logs onto the fire. Through the dark
backyard, my mother strides to the house
on two strong legs, she's going to fetch the *jāņu siers,*
yellow and dense, studded with seeds.
Just this morning she must have unpeeled
the cheesecloth, placed the loaves on platters.
To see her hurrying like she'd never
had an aneurysm. To see my father reaching
for the next bottle. Like the past wasn't banging
on the door of the house, wearing an SS uniform.

To see him pulling out the cork,
as if he had never, at eighty-five, opened that door,
and invited the war back in.

Just like the old times. Soon the neighbors will call
the police, now that the fire's so big, now that it's
midnight and the ancestors have arrived, armed
with their *kokles* and pranks. To see them jumping
over the flames, singeing the hems
of their *tautas tērpas*, folk garb, chasing each other
through the garden. To hear the songs
getting older, calling up the gods
of thunder and fire. To see Mr. K
feeling up Mrs. B, his big hand crawling
along her leg. To see my father checking out
the breasts on a Baltic beauty who's just arrived
from 1904, a basket of blackberries in her arms.

And that's the last straw. I slip into
the woods like I did as a girl after crawling
out my bedroom window. I run through the trees,
up the bank to the vacant lot where the boyfriend
sits in the car, smoking, waiting to take me out
of this nightmare, into his own American version,
his right hand on my thigh, the left handing me
the bottle of wine, the sweet kind that tastes
like blackberries, that makes me believe
there might be a heaven.

—11.10.2013

PRAYER 38

after Kurt Kren

now the sun & now the cloud & now

        the sideways snow

(begins) & sun again through birch trunks

        smacking down upon

the icy road (glancing off tire tracks)

        piercing eyelets

of frost behind

        the power line

when yesterday, so lavender

        so fringed (abandoned now)

produced this edgy wind (undid) the sun's nearly cleaving of

        (repeat, replay) the ice rink

glinting off some broken parts

(trailer hitch)

        as morning begins (again) (& did)

a pale come-on

in the east blue pubescent on the ridge

three clouds winking down

a flap of wing a fleck of rain

(a whim)

begins it on a tree

same tree mountain syllable grass face

(flit & shift)

& gone (behind) (chittering of the winter bird)

what sets this day apart

(from that one)   ?

with the floatplane taking off at nine

& nine & nine &

(this is how we tell time) a red truck

barreling down the lane every day

something

in its bed clattering (winter is deep now)

pray

slow it down slow

it down slow it

down when wind when light in indecipherable code

explain how to proceed

when sun a ruptured egg explodes

upon (the ground) this is it, this other dawn

asylum we lie

so thin upon

—11.12.2013

PRAYER 39

for Craig

You know the way it happens.
Branches intercept whatever's falling.

Each moment accruing
on the next adding weight until
it's heavy
as a mountain. But when it drops it's light

                as wind.

Then it's winter. A leaf turns white and fills
the sky with snow.

Tolstoy said *true life*
is lived when tiny changes occur.
We began as all things begin: you turned
toward me in the muskeg.
You showed me
a bog candle.

Nothing's been
the same since then.

                —11.15.2013

BOOK 4

Here, After

after a week of daily heavy snow I want to praise my roof

—Ellen Bryant Voigt

Walk to us, Jesus, through the walls of wheat
When our two tractors come to cut them down:
Sow some light winds upon the acres of our spirit,
And cool the regions where our prayers are reapers,
And slake us, Heaven, with Your living rivers.

—Thomas Merton

PRAYER 40

Loose hens early this morning. We herded them
through the orchard, discovered two ways
they could have escaped: ducking a gap
at the coop's base or bursting out
a tear in the mesh near the perch. If there's
an opening they find it. The dog at first seemed only
to exacerbate the hens' befuddlement and the chaos
of humans clapping, but in the end he chased the last idiot,
a rangy, skittish Arucana, straight in while we stood flapping
our arms yelling, "No, Boo, no." We slammed shut the door,
changed our tune to "Good dog." My love arrived,
climbed a tree to grab mangoes from the canopy with
a twelve-foot-long fruit-picker. He couldn't see the fruit
for the leaves so we stood below shouting "To the left,
to the right, up, out, toward the trunk, toward me" until we grew
exasperated, until we realized we had better things to do.
Simone Weil said attention is prayer and that's true. Every morning
I sit at the kitchen table watching for the first hint
of dawn with my pen in hand poised above paper waiting.
Sometimes it's broken— the thing that needs attending—
old rooster hopping on one good leg. That rooster can barely
walk yet he throws his head and crows and I say "You've still
got it, Wally." We left him outside last night by mistake.
Through the morning's rodeo he stood
immobile under the mango in tree pose.
My offering to him—a tiny pyramid of pellets, a pan
of water, this wasted day.

—12.2.2013

PRAYER 41

This is the story of the animal soul, not the divine soul.—Rumi

Rumi claims *the rational intellect should control*
the animal soul. In the predawn dark a cow across the gulch
bellows as though in answer. Mornings it's the domesticated
before the wild, the screech of African geese, the *chack-chack-chack*
of geckos in rafters, before any human sound, the beasts, common and
appearing placid, those of barnyard, coop and pasture voice
their longing as light comes on to tame them. Underneath the din,
the shush and rumble of ocean, constant reminder of origin.
Before they grow dumb in heat and sun, fowl and stock remembering
where and what they came from.

—12.3.2013

PRAYER 42

You poke your head through a window, which long ago
lost its glass to some punk who busted in to find
a dry place to drink his bottle of *kvass*. When he was done

he smashed his empty against the wall, in the house in Latvia
where your father was born. So the kitchen floor's one big midden,
shards keeping hidden evidence of your oma's life—birch ash

she scraped from the oven for tea to cure gout, three dead girls,
all named Lonīja (one drowned in a water trough), her poultices
and daily walks to Mass—leaving only facts of aftermath.

Last time you came to Kundzeniskis a scrap of lace curtain
still blew in and out as if to say, in Oma's porridge-thick
Changalisk dialect, *vot es te vel esmu*. Look, I'm still here.

A bird built a nest above the window. Now that nest's
mashed between frame and wall. Nostalgia's a waste here
but hard to kill as ticks or crabgrass. In another hundred

years some relation in its grip will stand beside the cellar
hole wondering where they went, your lost
Baginski clan. Erased, the caved-in house, which bespoke

some flawed seam in the genetic bedrock of that
peasant stock, some meth-skinny nephew who inherited
the homestead and let it rot. Of course it took more to undo

the gut and grit that built the house, birthed eleven kids
in the nearby *pirt*, that sunk the well, that plowed the rocky
earth, made it yield meat and sugar beets. It took war,

occupation, a family fleeing, it took history to break that will.
You stand here scheming projects for another century,
another country: greenhouse, chicken coop, doing over

what they did at Kundzeniskis. In this, you're no phoenix,
just the once knock-kneed kid who carries a tick under
her skin, making her want to dig, plant, spread manure,

build a ruin for the next generation. That tick, impossible
to kill, will outlast even the stone foundation, clinging to last
year's grass, waiting for some future cousin's sock to climb.

—12.4.2013

PRAYER 43

My love this morning trimmed
plants in the native garden.
I stood by pleading the case
of naupaka, sprouted from a mother bush
I found uprooted, half-dead
in the gulch last winter. There naupaka
grows wild, thick on a salt-smeared
slope the way it did when the first
Polynesians set sights on
these islands. Naupaka—succulent

green gleam skirting a steaming
newborn earth—watched them
make landfall. Seeds, eyeball white,
drooping like grapes, arising
from tiny stars. Atop points
along shore those dreamers
fixed routes to the next
island, navigated by celestial light, oceanic
current, bodies attuned as flight
feathers to slightest air torques.

I dragged that shrub up the cliff, clipped off
branchlets, dipped cut ends in hormone,
stuck them in pots and waited. It's what I do
best, living CT scan to scan, in three-month
increments. Cancer's come back to colonize
my lung's pleura. At night sometimes I feel

darkling cells coursing through
my bloodstream. Mystery of what's becoming
of my body carried day to day,
task to task. My love

trims the naupaka back to uncover
fragile coral 'ilima. *Stop,*
that's enough I beg. How unlikely,
survival. My lung feels quilted
since surgery, stitched with sinew, the body's new
mantra: *nothing belongs to you*, though
the impulse to say *this place*

is mine is strong. The neighbor fires up
his weed-whipper, razors down
grass along the electric fence line. The ocean's
voice is clear—this lull temporary, there's a swell already
being born in some Gulf of Alaska storm gyre.
Every native species arrived on swells, hitchhiked
on logs, was dropped by bird or wind, seeding home.

My love's put away his
hedge clippers. The sheep lie in their patch
of ironwood shadow. Between states
of resistance and surrender it's easy
to say I'm living in the now. Harder to
enact. Earlier the newborn
lambs ducked the fence-wire to nibble

endangered ohia and lama. Adorable, yes, but
I called the dog to chase them off.

It's a sheep-eat-native world.
The body chooses
what it fights for.

—12.5.2013

PRAYER 44

It was the autumn of the year

of the razor planted in the apple.

No child desires the apple, much less

the blade slid into flesh. Though we bite

    down, swallow core, pith, invisible

slit—the whole fable. Merle Jolls lived in the smallest house

on the street, green shingles blistered,

porch a-sag, lawn crabgrass-and

Queen Anne–laced. Recluse, he lent himself to our

rumors—long-bearded ancient, someone

said he grew potatoes in his basement. We believed.

It was the Halloween

    we ditched anything homemade for fear of poison—

Rice Krispie squares, fudge wrapped in wax paper. If you google

Merle Jolls, Silver Creek, you'll find

dates—born Nov 23, 1894, died eighty-five years later. Dig deeper,

you'll unearth how once he had

a missus, kin. According to Personal Paragraphs,

Lakeshore News and Times, May 23, 1946, they "called Sunday

on relations in Fredonia, Cottage, Buffalo,

and Springville." Rumi claims endurance

is flesh, or is it the other way? Imagine him

at eighty in green wool pants, hand disappearing

into paper bag to retrieve my treat, which I

sliced thin back home, just in case. This morning the world

is noisy with memory, lousy with self-defense. Imagine

his faith, hoeing tubers in the dark, imagine innocence—handing

apples out that fall. Imagine imagined danger.

The green shack is razed, Merle dead three decades. Being made

of bone and flesh, a myth

persists. Fear notwithstanding,

to the apple

I said yes.

—12.9.2013

PRAYER 45

You read about symptoms, short times to recurrence,
a year, two, maybe more to survive, all the while
finches prattle in the lantana, light spills onto floorboards,

pooling at your feet. It's linked, true, beginning
to end, whatever you search for you can find, shaded specifically
to your makeup—dire, hopeful, paranoid, skeptical, susceptible to

quackery, Pollyannaish, resigned. A dove coos, you shut your laptop,
take this insistence of birds and weeds to mean death's the mind's
cul-de-sac, while life is a trick of light, a persistence of

breeze sneaking beneath the sash
of the old window that will not shut.

                              —12.11.2013

PRAYER 46

Kurrr, kurrr, kurrr, kurrr, high or low, some variant mimicking
any number of birdsongs, *kur*, Latvian word for where.

This morning I hold *kur* in my hands like a prayer wheel,
give it a spin, *kur*, and its cousin *kas*—what?—who? Where

and what and who, my ancestors lifting
language from birds. Where shall you build

your nest, they asked, when, in
the displaced persons camp after World War II, the exiles

were handed papers: Canada? Buffalo? Trinidad? Commiserating,
heads together in the barracks, *Kur tagad?*

Where now? Unwilling migrants, my mother, my father, Cincinnati,
Chicago. Then skip, hop, skip, from Bronx

to Amherst to Silver Creek, New York. There they found
themselves accidentals, foreign, blizzard-blown

in the middle of a grape vineyard, mangling words, wearing
clothes the wrong way. Though something

of the landscape's grizzled hills did look familiar. My mother
took up birding, memorizing names of common species

at her feeder: nuthatchers (she called them), titmice,
chickadees, jays. Chased off voracious grackles, European starlings.

How many times removed am I, splintered from origins, over-wintering
like a plover on a Pacific island? *Kur, kur, kur?*

Kur-tu, kur-tu, kur-tu, the myna reiterates. Where, you, where
do you belong? Making the top one hundred of invasives, cousin

to my mother's hated starlings, ousting native owls, *pueo,*
from nesting holes. It's not their fault!

Some homesick someone brought them over, hidden
in her coat. On my first morning nēnē,

native geese, flapped over, calling softly, *nu, nu?* The way
my mother asked, when I migrated to Alaska, and now, and now?

What if you get stuck somewhere? Without proper shoes! Lost,
a storm blew the nēnē off Haleakala crater.

An energy healer tells me my cancer's lost, bumbled not
on purpose into my breast, seeking home. We make myth

and metaphor to explain where we came from, *vai ne?* It's all
anyone can do. The healer lays hands while I lie flat

on her living room floor. She delivers the news to my disease
gently: You don't belong here, *go-now, go-now.* At eighty-six,

my mother moved again, to Puget Sound, where nothing
outside her window is familiar, except maybe

the pigeons. When it's suppertime, she interrupts
our chatter, sending us away with her high-pitched,

two-note *at-ta*, bye now. We are homing.
No different than the myna, mimics to the end,

maps in hand, standing at the scenic lookout,
shouting, *kur tagad, kur tagad, kur tagad?*

Where now, where now, now where?

—12.12.2013

PRAYER 47

from Lake Erie floodplain I trace

my line my fate from oak fern nightshade

grackle woods & yellow crate of grapes

stacked at rows' ends from child-self

picking grapes talc dusted with

poison from Catholicism &

growing faint from

heatstroke migraine

sweat-stained midsummer combing grapes

eating grapes till

my mouth bled from sprayers

crawling down vineyards &

haze hovering all morning after

from concord juice my mother squeezed

through a sieve her quince

jelly her black bread her okra

cabbage her smoked pig

her mountain ash liquor jugged in the cellar

from my father's secondhand war terrors &

Marlboros & drinking bouts his birch switch flat of hand

belt slaps & ice-eyed danger face

from garter snake wild dog pack

railroad track & midnight

whistle of freight run to Buffalo

& fear of nuclear attack & house fire

& getting pregnant

from shale creek bed

warm water over ledge from

minnow jar & leg-hold trap

heat lightning wide-awake

hail & blizzard (lake effect) from ice storm

each branch glazed & deadly in morning

sun from nostalgia sick-sweet

as pesticide for that earth-flaw

where antique medicine bottles

spilled down ravine sides

with dumped tires & washing machines

to land in the oak-shady

creek bottom where all

my secrets are kept

—12.15.2013

PRAYER 48

for Asja

In predawn dark, a rat falling from a rafter is a dollop,
wind a whir, and suddenly I'm remembering my mother
teaching me to bake her hot water sponge cake.

How we whipped the egg whites with the electric mixer
until stiff peaks formed. How she warned me not to allow
a single thread of yolk to taint the white, or the cake

would fail. To fold white into yolk-sugar-flour was slow,
patient. She let me carve a wedge with the rubber spatula,
drop it to the batter's surface, then lift from the bowl's bottom

up and over the dollop, turning it in. Warned me
never to beat or mix or even stir—the cake would fall.
Once, dinking around, I stuck a wooden spoon into

the still-whirring beaters, bent the metal, splintered
the spoon into the batter. Once I cut her grandmother's precious
lace for a doll's clothes, and she cried, the savaged pieces

draped across her wrists. So many times I tried to shove
my peasant feet into her dainty pumps, hands into her evening
gloves. One spoon at a time, that first thin layer drawn across

the airy white forming a little hill. Folding only
just enough. The batter growing lighter by increments.
It was mostly space we folded in, taming down

the cloy. It was never so good as then, licked off
the finger, the cake itself, to me, disappointing, layers
smeared with homemade jam, topped with a stiff merengue.

Never so good as then, her instructing, trying to domesticate
my impertinence, teach me a little grace, me resisting,
the sweet on my tongue dissolving so easily

in that state of matter. Never so good as straight from
the Pyrex bowl. Never so gentle as the slide of batter
into an angel food pan. The rest up to her, what she

created from the baked version, brown on top and bottom.
Here I am, decades later sitting under the halogen
of a full moon, and that moment, which was many

folded into one, is so pure and specific, the sugar sharp
on my tongue, the spatula pushing as if through
an undertow. My mother taught me to fold. Never so

sweet as now. We were incorporating lightness
into a deep bowl. As some bird—probably an owl
out hunting—chacks its way across the lawn,

sounding like a key chain, and now the garden sprinkler
comes on, so I know it's 6:00 a.m. There's the first hint
of dawn slow-dissolving one more night. This is a fifty-

year-old love. It's heavy, so I fold in moonlight, the sound
of water spattered on leaves. Dim stars, bright moon—
our lives. The cake imperfect, but finished.

—12.17.2013

PRAYER 49

Half-moon through clouds moving west

No matter how thick or damp, within seven miles the dry air above Kapaʻa
absorbs every one

Sometimes wind flings rain in fistfuls across miles to pepper the skin
of a sweating runner

To the east, a manta shape of pale sky wanders in

Moonlight tints last night's puddles on the steps a shade of platinum she's never seen

She sits wrapped in a blanket, watching the moon the way she did an eclipse
as a child—through the mirror—sheen of water at her feet

Venus is brighter than the moon tonight

Her demons asleep in the imprint her head left on the pillow

The apostle Paul spoke of a *hope toward God* that is to her a hunger for every sound
the orchard offers

If she is, like the ritualized way day begins, in theme with variations

Recognizable to herself

If she is not merely repeating a litany of

If she is not herself a numbing repeating sequence of

If she is every day listening deeper with the body of

Working her limited vocabulary toward

Identifying the strange *wharrr wharrr* cry answering, three times,
the throat-song of the rooster

She is only repeating (not knowing) over and over, God's name—

rooster goose myna owl rat wind leaf dark rain morning moan star orchard cloud
rooster goose myna owl rat wind leaf dark rain morning moan star orchard cloud

If it isn't merely naming or a waiting to be struck and even if it is

A form of faith, this reaching toward

This laying down of hands blindly upon

The marks across her chest, her ribs, her neck, the scarred, the amputated

A form of love, even as it widens the gap within, the dark of

Being empty enough to absorb every breath of want because

Like those bearing clouds

The dry air absorbs wholly into itself

The reason for still being here

—12.23.2013

PRAYER 50

Farmers wait for the vegetal flush that follows
a night of rain. A teenaged girl wishes
for a tattoo of a semicolon to punctuate her wrist.
The known pain always easier than the unknown
possibles—someone said.

Wind—a sandpaper sound, recalls the word *curettage*.
The cumuli at midday break into
bits as though passed through a sieve, combed into
lesser parts. Like trying to tear darkness
into manageable chunks to write
a story you can live with.

The body is a garden, some say. No such thing
as disease. Cure hinges on belief. What to do with such
agency? *And if I die before I?* And if I fail? Pray?
(If the pessimism of the farmer, those might say,
then worm tracks blackening his yams, then
the empty water tank, then the cancer in his gut.)

The force of healing hard against
the force of reason hard against the force of need.

Would it have mattered if I'd had a child? Answer, little
unplucked fig. Uterus, you are no vessel of
emptiness, more a fist. Undetected on the latest
CT scan, declared surgically excised.
Dark pupil who tried and tried.

—12.26.2013

PRAYER 51

Lord, give me

something to believe

answers with a susurrus of swell, *shush now*, second-most

comforting sound

we know—out-breath

Give me—not the terrestrial

(distinct with plovers,

specific with ewes and ram

delineation of each asleep on its own territory of grass)

—give me ocean and drop cloth, cloud form shape-shifts

(someone night-gowned now draping

a wet silk, color of gill net,

of bottom fish skin over the sea)

leaving an imprint

the way a girl lays down a temporary tattoo,

examines the marks inside her wrist

Give me language for, language of

I believe in a shook sheet translucent and only momentarily

lucid this color assay, fog as it pulls and recedes

Give me an authentic

the sea is authentic as the ram who chooses one ewe

to mount while she grazes, after, he rests his chin on her back,

she shakes her ears, the sea authentic as

this day-lit observable world

the sea authentic means someone might misunderstand

look out her window and believe it's frozen

or from a viewpoint believe it's holding still

folding always into itself, the dark line

the sea's ambivalence

a smother, a caesura, phenomenon of lustrous smoke curve

(something about hurt here, and love)

a seep of purple, bluing into the shade of fabric softener

softer now, a yellowish-lichen-green swath appears

some lavender, *mutatis mutandis,*

needing to be changed *Lord, give me*

a stark white tropicbird slashing through,

a brightness stepping closer until embraceable

—12.31.2013

PRAYER 52

for Craig

This morning I would invent dew
heavy on grass, silvery patches bathing
our ankles as we walk & bananas ripe & fallen off their stalk

a basket of passion fruit & definitions of passion
& his big hands around my waist & his laughter against my throat

I'd invent a dream in which my love & I would stoke
a woodstove & the heat would dry the dampness
from our feet & we could take our sweaters off

& we'd wake & it would be the sun

—1.1.2014

PRAYER 53

New moon and lung ache, breath
to gather strength for what's not mine

to fight. In King Kam Park, boys light their last
sparklers. New moon, shut eye. The dark total

as I walk. *Talk me through the darkest part.*
New moon, Lord, my world tonight

out of hand. Far up, among stars dimmed
by volcanic smog, what used to be

a consolation. *Compose in darkness* said
the bard. Some darks the careful habits

shake off like flies. Leave me discomposed.
Lay the hard words across the grass.

Lay them down like lava rocks. Watch me
stumble through the dark.

—1.2.2014

PRAYER 54

You're sitting here, the table edge hard against
your knee, coffee residue a grit in your throat, scar-ache
dull beneath your bra strap. This is your body
solid and strong. North wind cool along the wrist bone.

You're sitting here but you're practicing for
not sitting here. So go ahead, imagine yourself into
the slump of jacket you left on the counter. A vase
without a bouquet, a leash that's lost its animal.

Imagine being a left-behind intention, castaway
to-do list with all its to-dos X-ed out. Absence deaf
to wind rattling a window pane, the neighbor's vacuum.
Shoes jumbled in a closet. Your mother's old

linens stashed in the cupboard uncoupled
from stories of origin. A dress a girl presses to her chest
in a thrift shop laughing, *imagine wearing this to prom.*
Be that gone. In Honokane Nui Valley, flash floods sweep

the bamboo grove in winter rains. Clumps of leaves catch
one side of each stem. Imagine being unseen evidence for
which way to run in case of flood. Water wanders
uncontained through ruins of aqueducts. Trees

cast heavy shade over abandoned taro plots. Hundreds
of people farmed here once, in full sun. Absence
can trade places. Imagine yourself into and out
of one of those places. Be part of all that's missing

from the earth today. Clouds parading before
an empty judge's stand. All the discarded plastic cups.
Coffee mug upside down on the rack.

—1.6.2014

PRAYER 55

The Japanese white-eye who eats my
mangoes is lovely, with his sweet *mejiro*—
eye-ring—pale against his olive face.
And he's monogamous, building his nest
of moss, lichen, hair, even spiderwebs.
What's not to like? In Asia, he's sometimes
kept for a pet. But here, displaced, he outcompetes
native birds for nectar. His sweet tooth
is insatiable. See my mango, neat cavity
jabbed into its meat? That's one version
of the white-eye's story. There's biology,
and there's survival.

Time is metaphor, a story we tell ourselves
to survive. For instance—my lung is a mango, cancer
a white-eye, trading flesh for absence.
My fate is a mango's. My flesh is a story's.
Time is a hoopskirt around my hips.
Metaphor is prayer. *Time, go with me.*
The white-eye's beak is tiny but sharp.
The mango's wound drips saffron juice.
Time is a mango. My life is a white-eye.
My story is a hoopskirt. My fate is sweet.
I eat a hole into it, bit by bit. Until all that's left
is the pit. I bury the pit in the yard.

—1.9.2014

PRAYER 56

for the other Eva

Water morphs into lavender spectrum.
I look away and color just happens. I look away
and the brassy moon has sunk into cloud bank.
I look away and lavender has mutated
into rotten ice in some wintry landscape,
grizzled mien of my youth, all the folded up
factories and bottling plants, sky coarse-grained
after ice storm, and here's

the linkage, the clinking into place, how this
subtropical ocean joins a frozen creek riven
between shale cliffs, my friend and I clattering
down rippled-in-place waterfalls on skates,
craving a less tame version of our givens—
polar explorers!—ducking when rocks come
clattering down around our earmuffed ears.

She was Estonian Eva. Like me, child
of exiles, kerchiefed grandmothers answering
the phone *I speak no English*, *Polka Varieties*
blaring in the background, black bread in
the fridge. Fathers smoking pack
after pack, imparting fear and prudence.
We went in for punk music, rendezvoused
with punks in pup tents. I swear we were
innocent.

I used to pray a lot then, kept up
a personal relationship to Christ, as in,
dear Lord, pleading that my cracked oboe

reed would mend, that my father not find out,
believing if I just believed enough, I'd achieve
any end. Dawn returns the real

to earth, and to the mind, harder colors,
blacker shadows. Now, when I fall to old
patterns, I'm aware of *dear Lords* snagging
in treetops, clicking in wind. Never reticent—
this mortal earth—cardinal, cane spider,
whale's chuff, memory of
treks more stumble than glide
over creek ice frozen rough
in its act of carrying across.

—1.15.2014

PRAYER 57

A girl sneaks a make-up mirror

out of the bathroom drawer, squats

on the lawn despite

what they say at school about blindness.

She tilts the glass toward the eclipse despite

her mother screaming stop.

Athabascans teach their children not to speak

dead-on of bears. If we name them,

their power will eclipse

night and day, animal and human, love

that strong tracking blood

across our sleeping backs.

What we didn't say

glints too bright for even my half-closed

eye. The unbearable

shine on the sheet-metal roof

of that barn, a blade of light sliding

its edge along each birch spine.

But if I never say it?

Say it: one word at daybreak: before this fades

to nothing, say it, before the body

melts like hoar in winter sun.

Before this frail

filament (back-lit a minute) falters,

scatters its seeds

all over the frozen pond.

—1.16.2014

PRAYER 58

is to climb on four limbs

is to grab branches, moss-grown

is to hand-hold crowberry sphagnum

is to dig heels into leaf-death

is to crawl up scree fall

is to pull the body into the saddle

    where anemones tremble

    in the southwest gale

is to go where plants are glossed

    by fog

is to go where grasses nod

    to what might be listening

    in that not-so-lonely place

is to ask

be with me when I fall

          —1.17.2014

So what is left for me
when what is left for me has come?

—Malachi Black, from "Vespers"

AFTER

She lay down upon rough low plants. Unbuttoned
blouse. Laid strips of moss across scalpel's track.
Gauzed, fern by fern, a glade upon. Shrouded
torso, eye to ankle, in swaths of fleabane, iris,
hellebore. Tattooed back in cranberry ink &
nettle-scratch. Body deconstructed by plant
& mineral, self replaced, cell by cell by soil
by water. Grafted onto earth's skin. Adorned finger
bones with bones of deer & marten. Mind changed into
mind of meadow. Accomplished in an eye-blink
when God's ruthless gaze turned a moment away
from Eden.

NOTES ON POEMS

Prayer 2: The photograph referred to in this poem is by the late Barry McWayne.

Prayer 6: With a bow to my friend and colleague Zack Rogow, whose workshop on Lorca and the concept of *duende* inspired this poem. The italicized segments are from Federico Garcia Lorca's *Theory and Play of the Duende*.

Prayer 10: Italicized line by singer-songwriter and friend David Lynn Grimes.

Prayer 11: This poem was inspired by Czeslaw Milosz's book *Facing the River*.

Prayer 16: "Make a fist for the heart" is from Lucy Brock-Broido's poem "Father in Drawer" in the December 2012 issue of *Poetry* magazine.

Prayer 17: The ʻōʻō bar is a Hawaiian digging tool, today, a long metal pole with a flattened blade on one end. The ancient Hawaiian version was a stick made of hardwood and used for turning over earth for cultivation.

Prayer 18: A further note on lava trees, from the Illustrated Volcano Glossary (volcanodiscovery.com): "When a liquid lava flow invades a forest, often, the lava does not overthrow the larger trees, but flows around their trunks. At the very contact of the hot lava to the bark, a thin layer of the lava is quenched sufficiently to form an isolating coating around the trunk. The tree itself most often burns down slowly, eventually falling down onto the lava. The typical lava trees are formed when after the initial surge, the lava level drains and lowers, but the earlier chilled coating around the trunk is left behind standing as a precise hollow cast of lava around the shape of the original tree up to the highest lava level during the eruption."

Prayer 23: With thanks to Malcomb, age three, for *moon, light, we*.

Prayer 29: Epigraph is from Letter 223 (to recipient unknown), from *The Letters of Emily Dickinson* (edited by Mabel Loomis Todd).

Prayer 34: On March 20, 2003, the United States invaded Iraq, launching the second Gulf War.

Prayer 38: I am grateful to my friend Michael Walsh, who introduced me to the poetry of avant-garde film, and to the work of Kurt Kren. This poem is inspired by Kren's 1975 film 31/75: *Asylum*.

Prayer 53: The italicized words "compose in darkness" are from "North" by Seamus Heaney.

BIOGRAPHICAL NOTE

Eva Saulitis, an essayist, poet, and marine biologist, has studied the killer whales of Prince William Sound, Alaska, for twenty-five years with her husband, Craig Matkin. Her first book, *Leaving Resurrection: Chronicles of a Whale Scientist* (Boreal Books/Red Hen Press, 2008), was a finalist for the Tupelo Press Non-Fiction Prize and the ForeWord Book Award. Her second non-fiction book, *Into Great Silence*, is from Beacon Press. A previous poetry collection, *Many Ways to Say It*, was published by Red Hen Press in 2012. A recipient of writing awards from the Rasmuson Foundation, the Alaska Humanities Forum, and the Alaska State Council on the Arts, she is an associate professor in the University of Alaska Low-Residency MFA program and a faculty member of the Kachemak Bay Writers' Conference.